love
in
bloom

vol 3

cheryl bradshaw

D1367862

for what haunts me
what guides me toward the light
and teaches me to love
i feel you
i feel you all

and to k.a.
for making
me believe again

you
have
to
do
your
own
growing
no
matter
how
tall
your
grandfather
was

—abraham lincoln

# FOREWORD

For those of you who have been following this series, you already know I have been writing poetry since I was in high school. Getting back into it this year has been good for both mind and soul. This is the third volume in the series, and with this one, the main themes are light, love, and being open to expand ourselves and our beliefs, whatever they may be. Sometimes it's these very things that are the hardest. And that's okay.

What I would hope for each of you is that you will take the time to understand yourself, what made you who you are today, and what your life is like because of it. We're all products of our history, but the beautiful thing is each of us has our own individuality. We have the chance to rise above the past and forge our own futures. We decide who we are and who we want to be, and I believe we're capable of this insight into ourselves at any time in our lifetimes, no matter how old we are.

I have enjoyed writing this series and hope to continue on to more like it in the future. In ways this feels like the beginning of what's to come, and I appreciate you for being right here with me. I am proud of what I've created and for the continued opportunity to shape my life, and I hope some of my poems have helped you shape yours.

May your lives be filled with peace and happiness, and may you always follow your bliss. For more of my scribbling, check out the other volumes in this series and follow me on Facebook and Instagram.

—Cheryl

# part one

## the
## darkness

the light
approached
the darkness
and said
*i do not wish*
*to live in the*
*dark anymore*
*i wish to live*
*in the light*
and though the
darkness chased
after her when
she turned to leave
he was
far too late
the light had
already slipped
from his grasp
falling into
love instead

— *the open crack*

# part two

# the light

farewell to the darkness
farewell to fostering my fears
and molding me into all
the things *you* wished me to be
i am strong now and as such
have no place in a world i
never quite fit into in the first place

*— don't lose sight of what is most precious*

the bird was perched
on a slim branch of
the tree his head cocked
to one side beady eyes
blinking down at me
with captive curiosity
i thought if i spoke to
him he might sing a
reply to me before
spreading his wings
and going on his way
but i didn't want to
spook him so i was
still and did nothing
and for a time we
did nothing together

— *i'll come for you*

i feel him
in the breeze
sometimes
even though
he doesn't
appear to
be there
or anywhere
really
except i
know he is

some days
the tiniest of
hairs stand up
on my neck
and it feels like
if i turned
even a little
in that
moment i'd
run right
into him

— *return to me*

when i was small
i used to imagine
myself living in
another dimension
because all my
life i've felt
i was born in
the wrong time
and place and
that my soul is
as old as time itself
humming and ticking
to the beat of the
footsteps of all
those who have
walked this earth
before me

— *generation gap*

he says he cannot accept me for who i am
and instead desires to change me into
a girl i wouldn't recognize if i saw her
on the street on the sunniest of days
i have no desire to be a spineless plaything
built on the hopes and desires of what
is required of me in order to remain

i wave farewell and skip away and
he seems confused because he's used to
getting his way and today he's learned an
important lesson about a girl with a mind
bright enough to understand what he's asking
*she's used to getting her way ... too*

— *i think therefore i am*

i used to feel shame in tears
in allowing such an annoyance
to rise within me until it poured
out of me making me weak
now it seems the weaker thing
was in betraying myself to
believe tears were a sign of
weakness when often times
their cleansing ability was
my greatest source of strength

— *floodgates opened*

there was a time i
shied away from
the noise and hustle
and bustle of things
now i walk the
lamp-lit streets at
night staring into
the varied faces
of beautiful
unfamiliar people
while breathing
in the fresh aromas
of the night air

it's colorful
and rich
warm and
wholly
intoxicating
and i want
to bathe
in it forever

— *strolling along the esplanade*

it is by my hand that i express
my most intimate inadequacies
the sides of myself i sometimes
see when i look in the mirror
and pretend aren't judging me
when i blink back at myself
i try to verbalize them out loud
but my thoughts don't string
together the way i'd like them to
which i suspect is because my
mouth is not as eloquent as the
quill which is a far sweeter thing

— playing my hand

i command
the element
of fire and
as such
i burn
from within
with a kind
of feverish
passion most
will never
see even
though it
boils just
beneath my
surface

— *zodiac*

i've always thought if
i were a color i'd be a
unique blend of two

part black
part pink

black for all the
times i've vowed
to never hurt again
and pink because
its softness never
allows the door
of my heart to
remain closed
for long

— *color theory*

creation is an inexplicable
thing often times leading
me to ponder my existence
and whether or not what i
think to be true actually is

questions sit at the forefront
of my mind until it opens
and can be examined through
thinking and reading and
feeling the world around me

there is much to explore yet

— *monkey see monkey do*

when you're not sure
which direction to go
turn your palms upward
and feel your existence

— *it came to pass*

once a closed
book i now
find myself
wide open

my pages
desiring to
be filled
with moments
and memories
and love
and life

— *all dusted off*

it seems i am at an impasse
a dash in time where all
has become clear to me
i reflect upon those who
have added to my life and
others who have routinely
sucked the marrow from my
bones until it has been
completely stripped of it

strip no more, suckers
your presence is no
longer required

— *plain as day*

do you begin the day in a
state of peace and calm or
do you peer out your bedroom
window frightened of what
the outside world represents

fear has no value or purpose
in the delicate corners of
your eternal soul and it wields
no power unless you let it

you are far too wise to be ruled by
something that doesn't even exist

— *master of your own domain*

fear is your mind creating imaginary
tricks of what's real and what isn't
why not create beautiful beaches
where playful puppies roam instead

— *miles of fluffy cocker spaniels named buffy*

sometimes
a single
full—bodied
breath is
all that's
needed to
make a
difference

— *ujjayi breathing*

if you shut yourself away from the world
how will you ever become all you're meant to be

— *star light star bright*

it is only by suffering
that we learn what we
must to survive so we
may then rise above it
rewriting the story
we assumed was
already well written

take the pen in your
hand and decide
what you want
to be written

— *the next chapter*

who is the one person
in your life you have
the most gratitude for
and does said person
know of his or her
value to you today

tell them … and if you
already have perhaps it's
time to tell them again

— *paying it forward*

there's a field
i visit where
i whisper my
innermost
thoughts aloud

it is here i
am wild and
free of those
who seek to
censure me

it is here
i learn to
love myself
even when
there's so
much of
me to
perfect

*— find your field*

it's amazing
what you can
feel when you
learn to open
your mind

— *fact or fiction*

many wander this
life as lost sheep

those who are the
leaders of the pack
are tasked with the
job of steering them
in the right direction

why, you ask

because even the
most wayward of
souls deserves a
helping hand from
time to time and
the resilient ones are
solid enough to offer it

— *a word to the wise*

don't waste a
single moment
on those who
feign friendship
and quickly plot
against you once
you've turned
your back

open your eyes
see what you're
meant to see

the blade of the
knife only stabs
in the back those
who aren't looking

— *sticky wicket*

give yourself
permission
instead of
always
exercising
restraint

freedom
is found
when taking
a chance
on yourself

— *self-discovery*

i embrace
the embers
the light
the fire
within me

after all …
there's nothing
quite like a
sinful crackling
blaze on a
blackened night

— *orbiting the sun*

asking forgiveness
is a sign we care
enough to let go of
a thing that should
have never occurred
in the first place to
someone far too
beloved to have
offended

— *olive branch*

when i was tossed
to the edge of the
earth and forced
to glance down at
the bubbling pit of
pained memories
and missteps taken
in my life the pit
beckoned me to
come closer and
then stretched itself
a little wider making
room so i'd slide in
perfectly when i took
the fateful plunge …

i teetered there
a moment
considering
just how easy
it would be to
succumb as i
had almost done
so many times
before …

a hand brushed
my shoulder and
when i glanced
back a familiar
face reached out
to me and said
*take it*
*do it now*
*hurry*
*we haven't much time*
there she was
just like she had
always been in
times like these
my constant friend
my pillar of light
appearing just in
time to steal me
away before i was
suffocated by
the darkness …

— *in the beginning there was a volkswagen cabriolet*

i hope for many things

one is to be the kind
of friend those inside
my personal bubble
have been to me

— *circle of friends*

there will
always be
times in life
when tossing
a dish across
the room and
watching it
shatter
seems more
satisfying than
bending a
humble knee
and maybe
sometimes the
breaking of a
thing that has
broken our spirit
needs to happen …

then again
anger never
endeavors to
share the road
with kindness

so pick a hand
which one do
you want to be

— *step on a crack*

is the person
you are now
the one you're
meant to be
or do you
hide yourself
behind a mask
of security
thinking you're
safe when the
truth is
pretending
you're someone
you're not
will never
be satisfying

— *picket fences*

time cares
not about
your regrets
in the end

by then it's
far too late
to make
peace with
your life

— *peace pipe*

don't fear the darkness
the darkness gives us the
strength to feel our way
to the door so we can
step through it and
sun ourselves on
the other side

— *an open and shut case*

the eyes reveal hidden mysteries
telling me everything i could ever
wish to know about a person
who he is and where she's been
and what he gets up to when he's
all alone on a brisk winter night

in these moments i find myself
wishing people could be as they are
instead of who they pretend to be
raw and honest and vulnerable
embracing themselves and the
spirit inhabiting their bodies

can you imagine what life would
be like if we could all be like this

— *cogito, ergo sum*

what is darkness anyway?
nothing more than a bully
without a spine with no
immediate place in your life

if you let him inside on a
whim the remedy is simple
open the door and toss
him back out again

— *auf wiedersehen für immer*

sometimes bad things happen
when we least expect it
the unknown creeps in making
us vulnerable and afraid of
what the future might bring
darkness is a seed without water

don't water it

— *chucking weeds out of my garden*

be bold and brave and strong and true to who
you are and who you have always wanted to be

seek to live a life free from the judgments of others
what matters most is your own efforts as a person

and if you find you're unsure of the way back to you
keep moving and seeking and toiling until you find it

— *it's out there, i promise*

remove the shackles in your chain
the ties that bind you and all that
seeks to hold you back from the
one you're meant to become

roam this earth and be free
there is no greater happiness
than a mind at peace

— *lay of the land*

the penny pincher pinched his pennies
until his jar of pennies was so full he
needed a bigger jar to keep them in

he thought about taking the trip of a
lifetime but decided it best to wait until
his jar was a bit fuller ...

time slipped away as it always does and
one day the man had lost his youth
his hair was thin and gray and his
height had reduced a full two inches

he had now amassed many jars of pennies
but being the prudent man he was he decided
it still wasn't time to spend them just yet ...

one fateful day the penny pincher passed away leaving
his loving wife to gather the jar of pinched pennies
with sadness in her heart she set off to see the world
she'd *waited* to see with her husband
and the penny pincher finally experienced
what he'd saved his entire life for
only now he had been reduced to a pile of ash
inside a dark tin box and was without the eyes to see it

— *what is the moral of this story*

the body
is like a
bottle of
fine wine
subject to
maturity and
fermentation
the longer
we use it

— *twist and bend*

you listen with your ears
but what do you really hear

you see with your eyes
but what do you gaze upon

you touch with your hands
but what is it you caress

you smell with your nose
but what do you find fragrant

you lick with your tongue
but do you really taste

are you living your life
or leaving it to waste

— *bigger better and brighter*

a soul is a delicate thing
stirring within the confines
of our fragile bodies
we're told it's eternal
and as such should be
nurtured and loved
*safeguarded*
and still we torment it
dragging it on a stick
along the dusty road of
our lives with little
regard to the damage
we're doing in the process
we are quick to forget
that a soul needs to
be nurtured in order
to survive

— *tlc*

have you ever been
pulled away from a
thing you thought you
no longer needed only
to find you longed for it
the minute it was absent
from your presence …

we all do it in ways
we learn to resist the things
we know in our hearts will
only hurt us in the end

the tricky part is learning
how to live without them

— *it is possible*

through our inner
spirit we learn to feel
learn to listen to our soul
directing us like the needle
directs the compass

— *are you listening*

in silence we learn
to see ourselves
for who we are
to embrace those
things about us
that have been
hidden within
the chaos and
the noise ...

in silence we
become whole
shedding the
previous version
of ourselves we
are free to become
become who we
wish to be next

— *don't fight it*

time is a love spanning our existence
it's the man working an extra shift
to provide food for his growing family
it's the woman who rises from bed to
reheat the meal for her man when he
gets home after his long day away
it's the child counting down the hours
until daddy arrives to tuck her in bed
and the dog wagging his tail as he stares
at the door in anticipation of his owner

time is many things to many people
how are you spending it

— *ribbon of time*

when the sooty ash rubs onto your
clean white shirt remember that if
you choose to surround yourself with
the dirty stains in life eventually you
will become tainted yourself
who you spend your time with is just
as important as how you spend it

— *stain stick*

if you could see yourself
as others see you what
version of yourself
would you see

someone who is happy
someone who is sad
or someone you fail
to recognize

— *selfie stick*

would the words
others use to
describe you
string along
like the
sweetness
of a love
poem or sting
like a bitter
bite of lemon

— *speakeasy*

in looking at ourselves plainly
we often see the harshest versions
of what we are today but we can
also see the gentleness of what
we may become if we but try

— *no one is perfect*

if all the air has been let out of your balloon
there's a tank of helium waiting for you
just around the bend and all you need
to do is to get there and fill it

— *take my hand*

you request my advice but when it's
given you lay out excuses like men
lined up in front of a firing squad
how then do you expect to learn
anything at all from me

— *burying the blindfold*

she sits at a table across from me
saying repetitive things like …

*i don't want to be alone again and*
*i know he loves me and we have*
*a bond only we understand*

and i'm left to wonder how
two people maintain a lasting
bond with the absence of trust

— *bonds don't work that way*

the dissolution of trust is like
a gun pointed at your head

it matters not because the
shot has already been fired

i should know
i've been there

what kind of life can be had
in constant suspicion of another

— *three blind mice*

sometimes the hardest thing to see
is the thing right in front of us

— *disappearing act*

if you want to know
what manner a person is
look into his eyes
(or hers for that matter)
gaze long enough
and all that needs
to be revealed will be

— *i see what others don't*

when you try to force a
square peg into a round hole
don't be surprised when the
peg splinters and breaks apart

no good comes from achieving
a thing by way of force because
force is what suits you best

letting a round hole be a round hole
and a square peg be a square peg
will lead to a much happier outcome

— *the birds have it figured out*

i know a girl
who thinks she's
found herself
and i don't
have the heart
to tell her
she hasn't
that what she
perceives to
be love is
nothing more
than a neatly
wrapped
lollipop with
a hollow
center ...

and so i love her
because in doing
so i believe when
the time is right
she'll look a little
harder at reality
than she is now
and one day she'll
figure it out for herself

— *walking on broken glass*

for those of you who are aggressive and difficult and the
kind of wild that leads to no good (you know who you are)

soften your hearts and learn to live with compassion instead
of struggling to survive with everyone including yourself

practice love and immerse yourself in how it feels to be
the kind of person others gravitate toward instead of
the one that makes them want to turn and run away

— *let go*

i wish she could see herself as i have always seen her
that she could strip away the outer shell of what
she tells herself is true and see what actually is
that she knew how much i've always admired her
for how different we are from one another and esteem her
for all the talents she has that i will always lack
like the way she dances across a room with so much grace
i'm moved to tears as i sit in the audience watching her ...

i wish she could understand i may not always say what's in my heart because i find the way i stumble over spoken words of depth and feeling so embarrassingly suffocating it stops me from speaking at all even though i should and while i'm not the loudest cheerleader i *am* the one who will always be here at the end of the night when she's been let down again and again and again by those who take all she has to give ...

i wish she could see that when she views
me as her harshest critic it's really me
pushing her to become the best version
of herself because she has more potential
than most and that at times i have stood
guard over her and been leery of some
of the company she keeps because i feel
more than she could possibly imagine …

i see the things she does not see and dream
the pain i wish was nothing more than an idle
nightmare even though in truth i'm aware
my visions of her are much too real for that
and so i take it on ...i take it all on myself
because what she can't handle i can and my
only way of protecting her is by keeping it in
and therein is my hope of shielding her from it ...

what she sees and feels is her own truth
my truth is much different and no less
real than hers but in this we are opposites
i have come to appreciate the uniqueness
of who she is which is far more appealing
than the degradation that comes from being
chastised for things not fully understood …

my priority has always
been and will always
be to stand guard over her
a constant protector
resolute and unwavering

— *the divine miss m*

you don't need to
seek my approval
you've always had it
you shouldn't feel
i'm not proud of you
i have always been
i may not possess the
gifts i wish i had or
know the right thing
to say when you
want me to say it
but i offer you the
gift of my words
the most valuable
assets in my possession

— *treasure map*

there isn't
always a right
way to say things
or a right way
to say them

to assume one's
opinion is the
only one
there is
removes the
other's ability to
see and feel
for themselves
in their own way ...

no two
interpretations
of a thing are ever
the same

what one feels
on one end is
entirely different
on the other

be mindful
when speaking
to those you love

words spoken
cannot be
taken back
i should know
i myself
am a repeat
offender

— *mysterious rants*

i am judgmental
and harsh and
hard to love

i am accepting
and kind and
easy to love

i am one
but i am also
the other

to love me
is to see both
sides of my
coin and
accept me
in spite of it

— *as i do you*

we are not the
same people
today as we
were yesterday
it would serve
those who
know us well
to let us out
of the box of
our past
and not to
judge us
for it

— *striving to be better*

is it right to judge
another for something
about which you are not
entirely sure whether
or not they is their fault
for example if you
believe you've been
slandered when
you haven't is it
any different than
passing judgment
on another before
giving one a chance
to speak for themselves

when you assume
before you know
you condemn
another with
prejudice

— *judge and jury*

i once knew a man
who was so covered
in sooty ash he could
no longer recognize
himself in the mirror
as he stood in front of it
which i expect was the
only prevention he had
against ensuring the
devil didn't smile back
at him when he did

— *the mirror has two faces, but you have just one*

the devious may
fool themselves
but they should
have no power
over fooling us
and so i ask you
is there anyone
in your life who
has no place in
your ascension
and if there is
such a person
pluck them out
and toss them
aside at your
earliest convenience

— *the earlier the better*

and now let's move to love
the most resplendent of all subjects

# part three

## love

the book was old
and weathered
and worn
and weary
it rested on its
side on an old
dusty shelf
a time capsule
left untouched
for decades

with tenderness
and care i slid
it toward me
and when i did
a letter slipped
out from within
its delicate pages …

i plucked the
letter off of
the ground
inspecting it
in my hand
the outside
was crusty
tarnished
and spotted
with tiny
circular stains

a name had
been inked
in eloquent
calligraphy
on the front
and was
addressed
to a woman —
genevive …

i hesitated
before i
opened it
because i
was not
genevive
and it felt
as though i
would be
invading
her privacy
somehow
by reading it ...

when my
curiosity
took over
as it often
did in times
like these
i slid my
finger into
the crease
my eyes
feasting
on the words
before me ...

*all my life*
*i've never met*
*a woman like you*
*please genevive*
*if you really love*
*me as you say you do*
*don't marry him*
*marry me*

*all my love*
*gareth ...*

i walked to the
reception desk
and posed the
following
question to
the elderly
woman behind
the counter:
*where did the*
*books in my*
*room come from*

her reply
*why do you ask*

i presented her
with the letter
and she slid a
pair of round
spectacles over
the ridge of her
nose and held it
in front of her ...

*did you read it*
she asked
i nodded

*and what would*
*you like to know*

*did genevive*
*choose gareth*
*in the end*

she smiled and
then lifted a
long slender
finger in the
air and pointed
at a portrait
of a couple
behind me
*that's genevive*
*and gareth there*
*and i am their*
*daughter*

— *the enchanting tale of genevive and gareth*

love
is
a
smile
from
a
stranger
after
a
hard
day

love
is
a
trusting
baby
squeezing
her
hand
around
my
pinkie
finger

love
is
the
woman
holding
the
elevator
when
i'm
still
ten
feet
away

love
is
cookies
left
on
my
doorstep
without
a
note
or
a
reason

love
is
the
way
the
night
stars
seem
even
shinier
when
i'm
with
the
one
i
adore

love
is
a
phone
call
from
my
daughter

love
is
a
kind
word
from
my
mother

love
is
a
stranger
asking
about
my
life
when
he
knows
nothing
of
it

love
to
me
is
all
these
things
and
more

what
is
love
to
you
?

— *you & us*

i wanted to learn how
to breathe again so i
went to the ocean in
search of what i
thought i had lost
when i stood beside
him and stared into
the distance somehow
it seemed better …
different and brighter
than all the times before
or maybe it was me
who was different …
finally looking a
few feet ahead
instead of always
staring through
the same old
dusty telescope

— *20/20 vision*

i opened my eyes and there
he was standing before me
like he'd been there all along
i just needed to open my
eyes a bit wider to see him

— *hi … what's your name*

my experience of
love is as vast as the
mysterious universe
in which we live
i've loved thin and
i've loved deep
and sometimes i
haven't loved at all
i've given my heart
and taken it back
and locked it away
when i was too afraid
to let it run free ...

my history of love
is like multiple
forks in the road
each representing
a path i've traveled
when it suited me

nothing is more
beautiful than
finding the one
who suits me best

— *exploring my options*

seek after
the one
who enters
your life
and alters
your identity
without trying
to make you
anything but
the best version
of who *you*
have always
wanted to be

that one there
is the keeper

— *the right fit*

be
the
kind
of
person
you
would
love
if
you
met

— *hello there*

he was pretty
and his soul
was even
prettier
and i
wanted
nothing
more than
to immerse
myself in
it forever

— *shiny and new*

real love is
more than the
combination
of two souls
coming together

it's a daily
journey
growing in
sweetness
over time

— *honor and cherish*

when he enters the room
there is much i want to say
but too often i struggle to say it
the sight of him stirs my soul
like an intoxicating sip of wine
when it first touches my lips ...

maybe that's why i'm
always so breathless

— *the sweet escape*

percy the persnickety
penguin feasts his eyes
along the beach in search
of just the right pebble
which he presents to
his one true love as part
of their budding courtship
if accepted a bond is formed
for an entire lifetime

i can think of far little
sweeter than that

— *lady's choice*

there's a kiss and then there's
something entirely different
a kind of tender embrace that
leaves you feeling like you
have just been devoured in
the best possible way

— *dessert before dinner*

before the
twain had
met they
asked

*why is he special*
*what makes him*
*different than*
*everyone else*

my reply
was simple
*when you*
*see us together*
*you'll know*

— *anomalous*

his body is like
a map of places
i've never been
creases and lines
stalwart and
yet rhythmic at
the same time

and i find
myself wanting
to explore all of it

— *studying abroad*

when i leave this
life i will leave it
knowing that when
i loved i loved to
the fullness extent
of what i was
capable to give
that i found
someone worth
every moment
i spent shaping
myself to get to

— *tree house in the sky*

when the door closed
behind me and i found
myself missing him
even though he was
mere moments away
i knew what i felt
for him was different
than anything i'd
experienced before

— *the moment you know*

have you ever fit so perfectly next to another person
the shapes and contours that blend your bodies together
connect like you were created at the same time

— *kinetic energy*

sometimes
when he sleeps
i stay awake
a few moments
longer just
to breathe in
the wrap of
his embrace

— *counting sheep*

the sparrow flew
far from home
searching for the
part of her she
always felt
was missing

what she found
was not at all
what she expected
it was in fact
infinitely better

— *life at its best*

the map of his body
had the most beautiful
carvings and creases
it told me he had been
somewhere interesting
and all i could think of
was what my own might
be like if i'd gone with him
saw as he did through
his eyes and felt what
touched his soul

— *complementary differences*

isn't it interesting when
two very different
journeys connect
and become one

— *connect four*

my heart is like the
strings on a guitar
play the melody right
and it's yours forever

— *drawer left open*

the heavy awkward
thing slipped from
my buttery hands
clattering onto the
soiled ground below
i looked up expecting
to be scolded because
a good scolding was
what i had grown used
to from another in my life
(one i had sent through
the exit door for crimes
of avarice among
other things) …

he blinked at me
in confusion and
when i began to
apologize his face
softened and i saw
a kind of genuine
compassion i had
come to believe
was a thing of
myths and legends
of the way a people
used to be with
one another and
not the way they
were now ...

i stared back
at him thinking
that for the
first time in
a long time
i actually felt
safe again

— *keep paddling*

it's nice to know a thing still exists
in this world when you think it extinct

— *predilection*

his kiss is
like the
petal of
a rose
soft and
provocative

sometimes
i almost
forget to
breathe
because of
how utterly
consumed
i am
by it

— *all wrapped up*

it seems to
me now that
whatever i
thought i
was looking
for all paths
circled back
to you

*— ferris wheel*

it used to be
that i wanted
nothing more
than to keep
the most
intimate parts
of myself
hidden

but with
him i want
to peel
myself
apart

— *bare*

genuine
affection is
laughing with
someone when
they laugh
and weeping
when they
need to weep
it's being there
even when there's
somewhere else
you're meant
to be and
knowing there's
nowhere on
earth you'd
rather be than
where you are
right now

— *the nurturer within*

it's interesting how our
interpretation of love
changes when we meet
someone who is infinitely
more than all the others
who have gone before him

— *bright sunshiny day*

there's a pair of throw pillows in my
hotel room with black and white abstract
birds on the front that appear to have been
drawn by a child in elementary school
the birds are in a grassy field surrounded by flowers
basking in the sun as it shines down on them
and though they could be immersed in their garden
paradise they're turned toward each other
like all they care about is being together

— *side by side*

i watched a man
gaze at his loving
wife of more than
forty years like she
was still just as
spellbinding and
alluring to him
as she had been
on the day they
first met …

and i pondered about why
so many lovers bicker
and fight with the one they
should hold most dear

why do we treat those
we cherish worse than
the beggar on the street

why must we bicker

appreciate what you have
while you still have it
one day the love of your life
will be gone and it will be far
too late to make amends by then

— *needle and thread*

why not instead say things to your lover like ...

*the wind whispered your name through
the trees and it blew me back to you*

*my life was incomplete until you arrived
at my doorstep and now i am complete*

or how about something easy ...
*i thought of you today and it made me happy*

— *use your words*

i've lived many a blissful night alone
but when we are parted i cannot imagine
how i survived existence before you were in it

— *the twain shall meet*

have you ever looked to the heavens and
seen a cloud in the shape of a heart and
it reminded you of someone … i have

— *spiraling staircase*

i think the thing
i've always wanted
most is the kind of
person who sees more
in me than everyone
else ... more than i
see in myself even

the kind of person
i'm not afraid to
be myself with
one who loves me
flaws and all

the kind of person
who places value
on a love that's true
one who makes
me want to strip
myself bare so he
knows me inside
as well as out ...

the kind of person
i want to run to
instead of one who
makes me run away

the kind of person
i would sacrifice
for because he's
a sacrifice
worth making

— *inner beauty*

when your heart is ripped
from you and you watch it
pulse slower and slower
until it stops beating you
may decide you aren't
capable of ever feeling
real love again but you
would be wrong

the heart is far more
capable than you think
and though the pool of
worthy suitors is shallow
it still contains water

— *swimming upstream*

give me precious
moments of time
your innermost
thoughts and the
depth of your soul
and i will give
you all of me

— *to infinity*

it's when we're not looking
that life throws us the biggest
curve ball of them all and the
best part is when you're where
you need to be so all you have
to do is to reach out and catch it

— *glove in hand*

he said he wanted to know
the one thing about me
that i only knew myself
the thing i'd never told
anyone until now
the kind of deep dark
secret i pushed back
inside whenever it tried
to bubble to the surface

and though i'd become
an expert at making
sure the floodgates
remained closed i found
myself wanting to tell
him everything

— *open book*

i watched the fragile aging man
step away from the car close the
door and plant his cane on the
ground in front of him

inch by inch he made his way
to the other side while the
woman sat in the passenger
seat and patiently waited

when he opened her door
they smiled at each other
and he extended his hand
and i saw what lasting
love looked like

— *wedded bliss*

sometimes in my most quiet moments
i think of him while he's away and
wonder how i got so lucky

— *finders keepers*

the moment the butterflies
hit and you realize you
feel something more than
you've allowed yourself
to feel for anyone in a
long time is the scariest
part because actualization
makes you vulnerable

vulnerability involves risk
which leads to a question
of investment and how
much of yourself
you're willing to give

sometimes when the
stakes are high the
reward is even higher

— *jackpot*

the moment my heart races
like a roller coaster ride
that never slows down
i know i'm smitten

— *bang the drum*

i've entwined with bodies before
but never one as lovely as his

— *keyhole*

the difference with him is
when i talk he actually listens

— *hearing aid*

we met when our
hearts had budded
finally beginning
to open again
and neither of us
seemed to be sure
what we were
capable of at first

i remember having
the strangest feeling

those before him had
tried making their way
inside but few had
succeeded on a
marginal level
and for a long while
i had thought myself
incapable of ever
loving again …

somehow he managed
what others had tried
to achieve and failed
the moments were
slow at first but
moments nonetheless
and after so much
time feeling nothing i
was scarcely aware
of what was happening
to me when
it happened

but it *had* happened
i was no longer
closed and when
i finally embraced it
my entire world
became different

— *metamorphosis*

i look back at those i
thought i loved when i
didn't even know what
love was and realize
what i was feeling at
the time was a version
of affection but
wholly incomplete
a love in progress
a simple attachment
that achieved the
purpose it needed to
achieve at that time …

what seemed like love
was often disguised
as what it really was ...
a casual affection
and sometimes
not even that
sometimes it was
more of a placeholder
i found myself in
before banging on
the door to get out

love has altered me
over time as i
expect it has
altered you
and i hope you
have learned
to cherish it
as i have

— *gemstone*

you are          loved you
are loved you       are loved you
are loved you are    loved you are loved
you are loved you are   loved you are loved you
are loved you are loved you are loved you are loved you
are loved you are loved you are loved you are loved you are
loved you are loved you are loved you are loved you are loved
you are loved you are loved you are loved you are loved you are
loved you are loved you are loved you are loved you are loved you
are loved you are loved you are loved you are loved you are loved
you are loved you are loved you are loved you are loved you
loved you are loved you are loved you are loved you are
loved you are loved you are loved you are loved you
are loved you are loved you are loved you are
loved you are loved you are loved you are
loved you are loved you are loved you
are loved you are loved you are
loved you are loved you are
loved you are loved you
are loved you are
loved you
ARE

# THE END

# ABOUT CHERYL BRADSHAW

Cheryl Bradshaw is a *New York Times* and *USA Today* bestselling author writing in the genres of mystery, thriller, paranormal suspense, romantic suspense, and poetry. Her novel *Stranger in Town* (Sloane Monroe series #4) was a 2013 Shamus Award finalist for Best PI Novel of the Year, and her novel *I Have a Secret* (Sloane Monroe series #3) was a 2013 eFestival of Words winner for best thriller. Since 2013, seven of Cheryl's novels have made the *USA Today* bestselling books list.

# BOOKS BY CHERYL BRADSHAW

**Sloane Monroe Series**

Black Diamond Death (Book 1)
*Charlotte Halliwell has a secret. But before revealing it to her sister, she's found dead.*

Murder in Mind (Book 2)
*A woman is found murdered, the serial killer's trademark "S" carved into her wrist.*

I Have a Secret (Book 3)
*Doug Ward has been running from his past for twenty years. But after his fourth whisky of the night, he doesn't want to keep quiet, not anymore.*

Stranger in Town (Book 4)
*A frantic mother runs down the aisles, searching for her missing daughter. But little Olivia is already gone.*

Bed of Bones (Book 5)
*Sometimes even the deepest, darkest secrets find their way to the surface.*

Flirting with Danger (Book 5.5) A Sloane Monroe Short Story
*A fancy hotel. A weekend getaway. For Sloane Monroe, rest has finally arrived, until the lights go out, a woman screams, and Sloane's nightmare begins.*

Hush Now Baby (Book 6)
*Serena Westwood tiptoes to her baby's crib and looks inside, startled to find her newborn son is gone.*

Dead of Night (Book 6.5) A Sloane Monroe Short Story
*After her mother—in—law is fatally stabbed, Wren is seen fleeing with the bloody knife. Is Wren the killer, or is a dark, scandalous family secret to blame?*

Gone Daddy Gone (Book 7)
*A man lurks behind Shelby in the park. Who is he? And why does he have a gun?*

\* \* \*

## Sloane Monroe Stories: Deadly Sins

Deadly Sins: Sloth (Book 1)
*Darryl has been shot, and a mysterious woman is sprawled out on*

*the floor in his hallway. She's dead too. Who is she? And why have they both been murdered?*

Deadly Sins: Wrath (Book 2)
*Headlights flash through Maddie's car's back windshield, someone following close behind. When her car careens into nearby tree, the chase comes to an end. But for Maddie, the end is just the beginning.*

\* \* \*

## Addison Lockhart Series

Grayson Manor Haunting (Book 1)
*When Addison Lockhart inherits Grayson Manor after her mother's untimely death, she unlocks a secret that's been kept hidden for over fifty years.*

Rosecliff Manor Haunting (Book 2)
*Addison Lockhart jolts awake. The dream had seemed so real. Eleven—year—old twins Vivian and Grace were so full of life, but they couldn't be. They've been dead for over forty years.*

Blackthorn Manor Haunting (Book 3)
*Addison Lockhart leans over the manor's window, gasping when she feels a hand on her back. She grabs the windowsill to brace herself, but it's too late——she's already falling.*

\* \* \*

## Till Death do us Part Novella Series

Whispers of Murder (Book 1)
*It was Isabelle Donnelly's wedding day, a moment in time that should have been the happiest in her life...until it ended in murder.*

Echoes of Murder (Book 2)
*When two women are found dead at the same wedding, medical examiner Reagan Davenport will stop at nothing to discover the identity of the killer.*

* * *

## Stand-Alone Novels

Eye for Revenge
*Quinn Montgomery wakes to find herself in the hospital. Her childhood best friend Evie is dead, and Evie's four—year—old son witnessed it all. Traumatized over what he saw, he hasn't spoken.*

The Devil Died at Midnight
*When true—crime writer Alexandria Weston is found murdered on the last stop of her book tour, fellow writer Joss Jax steps in to investigate.*

Hickory Dickory Dead
*Maisie Fezziwig wakes to a harrowing scream outside. Curious, she walks outside to investigate, and Maisie stumbles on a grisly murder that will change her life forever.*

Roadkill
*Suburban housewife Juliette Granger has been living a secret life … a life that's about to turn deadly for everyone she loves.*

\* \* \*

## Non-Fiction

Arise
*Arise is a collection of motivational stories written by women who have been where you may find yourself today. Their stories are raw, real, heartfelt, and inspiring.*

\* \* \*

Poetry

Love in Bloom poetry collection (3 volumes)
*These delicate, heartfelt poems allow you to explore the raw, heartfelt emotions we all experience in life—joy, sorrow, confusion, and above all … love.*

CPSIA information can be obtained
at www.ICGtesting.com
Printed in the USA
LVHW031948240120
644729LV00002B/276